Before You Jump The Broom:

Clean Up Your Room

Rev. Dr. Alfonso Wyatt and
Ouida C. Wyatt

Copyright © 2014
Rev. Dr. Alfonso Wyatt and
Ouida C. Wyatt
Before You Jump The Broom:
Clean Up Your Room
Printed in the United States of America
ISBN 978-0-9904624-4-6

All rights are reserved solely by the author. The author declares that the contents are original and do not infringe on the rights of any other person. Unless otherwise indicated, Bible quotations are taken from the New International Version of the Bible. Copyright © 1973, 1978, 1984 by Biblica. Proverbs are from The Message Bible.Copyright © 2002 by Eugene Peterson. Used by permission. All rights reserved. No part of this book may be reproduced in any form except with permission from the author. The views in this book are not necessarily the views of the publisher.

Broom design- Ouida C. Wyatt
Photo credits - Anew Photography

Before You Jump The Broom:

Clean Up Your Room

Also by Alfonso & Ouida Wyatt

Soul Be Free Poems Prose & Prayers

Soul Be Free II

Mentoring From The Inside Out:
Healing Boys Transforming Men

Website: www.strategicdestiny.com
Email: alfonsowyatt09@gmail.com
Twitter: @AlfonsoWyatt2

*For couples
on the journey
of writing
the lyrics
to their
love song.*

Table of Contents

Preface…………………………………………..9

Vows……………………………………….13

Marriage Questionnaire…………………...17

Foundation Truths……………………...25

Anger: Sweet or Sour……………………....35

Marital Math……………………………41

Afterword…………………………………47

Biographies………………………………..51

Preface
Rev. Dr. Alfonso Wyatt

Before You Jump The Broom: Clean Up Your Room is not just a catchy book title, it is sound advice. I have conducted many weddings and sometimes it seems there is more thought and preparation for the wedding day than for the marriage. With that in mind, my wife and I have endeavored to combine practical wisdom gleaned from four decades of marriage and friendship to share with couples. Throughout the book, you will find invaluable scriptural insight contained in Proverbs to add a needed spiritual foundation. We love to laugh so you will notice that we did not leave out humor.

A good, strong, lasting marriage takes hard work, consistent attention, and proactive communication. We hope that you will apply these same qualities while you read and share this work. It is our fervent prayer that couples contemplating spending their lives together will find *Before You Jump The Broom* an important tool and vital resource throughout their marriage. Please take advantage of the blank note pages after each section to capture your thoughts and notes to self.

Well-spoken words bring satisfaction; well-done work has its own reward.

Proverbs 12:14

Beloved, it is fitting that we start this book with the sacred pledge that is foundational to marriage. The vows are not a contract with two people, but a sacred covenant between two people. Take a long look at the pledge you will soon say to your fiancée. These are more than words on a paper, but a solemn vow that is not to be entered into lightly…

Vows

I take you to be my lawfully wedded spouse, my constant friend, my faithful partner and my love from this day forward. In the presence of God, our family and friends, I offer you my solemn vow to be your faithful partner in sickness and in health, in good times and in bad, in joy as well as in sorrow. I promise to love you unconditionally, to support you in your goals, to honor and respect you, to laugh with you and cry with you, and to cherish you for as long as we both shall live.

Knowing what is right is like deep water in the heart; a wise person draws from the well within.

Proverbs 20:5

MARRIAGE QUESTIONAIRE

The act of marriage is one of the most sacred commitments that a human being can make by sharing his/her: self, dreams, hopes, good parts, not-so-good parts, pain, joy and fortune with each other. It would be unreasonable to think just because you love each other that there will not be adjustments or disagreements. This survey was created to help couples have a meaningful dialogue on key aspects that may have an impact on their marriage. Your task is to answer the following questions individually then compare your responses when you both have completed the assignment. Remember, the deeper you go the more you will grow. Feel free to use the blank pages provided to capture your thoughts. After completing this assignment, you may be inspired to form your own questions to present to your mate.

1. What has been the biggest change in you since your relationship started? What, in your opinion, has been the biggest change in your fiancée?

2. What are the three most important ingredients for a healthy marriage (put your response in order of importance to you)?

3. It is now 20 years from your wedding day, describe your marriage from this vantage point: Where do you live; where are you working; how many children do you have; what has your partner accomplished (this is really

your time to present your "vision" for the marriage) that pleases you; what one word captures this period in your life?

4. What is the one issue that you know you have not yet fully discussed or resolved that you have placed on the "backburner" of your soon-to-be shared marital stove?

5. What person/role model, past or present, real or fictional, best epitomizes what a good and lasting marriage means to you (please state why)?

6. If you can give your spouse a gift (not money) that you know deep down inside he or she needs and deserves, what gift would you offer?

7. Please write in the space below any question(s) on your mind that you wish your spouse-to-be would answer.

Before You Jump The Broom: *Clean Up Your Room*

NOTES

> We plan the way we want to live, but only God makes us able to live it.
>
> Proverbs 16:19

Seven Foundational Truths for a Strong Marriage

My wife and I have been together for 40 years and have learned through insights, mistakes and revelation, vital truths along the way. Here are hard-earned truths that can create meaningful healing marital dialogue and a stronger relationship.

1. **Fight For Peace Rather Than Fighting Each Other**—If you are going to fight (argue) learn how to fight fair: no sneak attacks; no dropping 'hurt' bombs; no lying-in-wait for an ambush; no backstabbing. Know when to "surrender." Never force each other into the position of defending the indefensible—it is always a "no win" situation.

2. **Being Understood vs. Being Right: Which Is More Important?** —This is a choice each couple has to make on a daily basis. One leads to possible reconciliation and the other leads to a legalistic exercise of keeping tally of points to prove who is right. This encourages listening for inconsistency or "pounce points" to make a swift rebuttal rather than listening for an opportunity to address real issues.

3. **Effective Communication Is More Than Getting Your Point Across**— Conversation is a multilevel process that involves the eyes, body, ears, emotions—and the past (both known and hidden). This is what makes effective communication difficult because sometimes a person can be talking and the other person is

hearing another voice in his/her head. This phenomena creates AM (All Male) and FM (Female) communications. One party is broadcasting on one frequency but not heard on the other frequency.

4. **WARNING: Don't Push The "Crazy" Button**—You know what buttons to push that drives your partner over the edge. If you push that button and your partner retaliates by pushing your button, you now have grown-ups becoming proficient at playing games like: the silent treatment or, I am going to hurt you just like you hurt me.

5. **PRAY vs. PREY**—Do you pray for one another (together & separately) or do you prey on one another? One

definitely helps and the other surely hurts. Prayer may not always change the situation immediately but it will always change the person in the situation. Pray not to prey…

6. **"Out" Is Not The First and Only Option**—Every couple will have disagreements because there is no such thing as a perfect marriage. If the threat of leaving/ending the marriage is the first and only response to problems, large or small, the opportunity for resolution is lost in threats rather than found in solutions.

7. **<u>Watch Out For Direct/Indirect Anger</u>**—We all get angry because we are human. Anger can be productive if it leads to a viable solution. On the other hand, anger can fester and explode; anger can be avoided; acted out, or it can be swept under the proverbial rug; or internalized which can lead to depression.

NOTES

Words kill; words give life; they're either poison or fruit—you choose.

Proverbs 18:21

What is Your Expressed Anger of Choice? (Sweet or Sour)

1. Bitter Honey: From past, present or future you cannot or will not let it go.

2. Red Hots: Every situation garners the same heated response.

3. Twizzlers: There is always some twisted logic to how things appear.

4. Peanut Brittle: You are held together by all the slights—real or imagined.

5. M&M's: Mean messenger; it is not what you say but how you say it.

6. Pay Day: Retail Therapy: You spend as a way of getting even.

7. Star Burst: The outside looks squared away then here comes fireworks.

8. Mounds: Key issues and concerns are constantly swept under the rug.

9. Sweet Tarts: Being emotionally unpredictable: nice/nasty.

10. Snickers: Mocking a person's sincere attempt to respond to a problem.

NOTES

Without good direction, people lose their way; the more wise counsel you follow, the better your chances.

Proverbs 11:14

Marital Math

+) Couples can add significantly to their ability to grow together and move forward in a mutually positive direction by staying focused on the fruit of the spirit love, joy peace, patience, kindness, goodness, faithfulness, gentleness and self-control.
(Galatians 5:22-23)

—) Couples must know what to subtract from their marriage—anything that steals love or respect must be extracted; anything that kills peace of mind must go, and anything that destroys trust must be eliminated.
(John 10:10)

÷) Couples must be careful how they divide responsibilities, money, time, attention and intimacy. An imbalance, either conscious or unconscious, can throw off the marriage. While the division in marriage is not always equal, it should always be fair so there is equal joy in sharing dividends.
(Mark 3:25)

X) Couples can multiply the power in their marriage by consciously multiplying their strengths and not multiplying weaknesses.
(Joshua 24:10)

Before You Jump The Broom: *Clean Up Your Room*

NOTES

Souls who follow their hearts thrive; fools bent on evil despise matters of soul.

Proverbs 13:19

AFTERWORD
OUIDA C. WYATT

People often ask what is the secret in keeping it together for 40 years? The real answer is; it is hard work keeping promises that are made; however, it is possible to do. A quote from our book <u>Soul Be Free II, Poems Prose & Prayers</u> speaks to the above question:

> "The same love people write about, sing and yearn for can turn to hatred when not properly respected, caringly protected, or truthfully corrected."

The thing I know for sure is that God is and has been our divine navigator through thick and thin. As a final thought, I would like to share the lyrics to a hymn that is close to my heart: *It Is No Secret What God Can Do,* C. S. Hamblen

> The chimes of time ring out the news, another day is through. Someone slipped and fell. Was that someone you? You may have longed for added strength your courage to renew. Do not be disheartened, for I bring hope to you.
>
> There is no night for in His light, you never walk alone. Always feel at home, wherever you may go. There is no power can conquer you while God is on your side. Take Him at His promise, don't run away and hide.
>
> It is no secret what God can do what He's done for others, He'll

do for you. With arms wide open, He'll pardon you. It is no secret what God can do.

Beloved, a year from now go back to your vows and read them aloud to each other—stay the course for love never fails.

Love is patient, love is kind. It does not envy, it does not boast, it is not proud. It does not dishonor others, it is not self-seeking, it is not easily angered, it keeps no record of wrongs. Love does not delight in evil but rejoices with the truth. It always protects, always trusts, always hopes, always perseveres. Love never fails.

1 Corinthians 13: 4-8a

BIOGRAPHIES

Photo taken by **Theodore Coln**

REV. DR. ALFONSO WYATT is a renowned public theologian, role model, mentor and national speaker on issues that impact children, youth, families and community health. He is an advisor to government, universities, public schools, community-based organizations and civic groups. He is an Ordained Elder on the ministerial staff of The Greater Allen AME Cathedral of New York. He has designed innovative workshops, retreats and seminars for church leaders, men, youth ministries and married couples. Alfonso Wyatt attended Howard University, Columbia Teachers College,

The Ackerman Institute for Family Therapy, Columbia Institute for Nonprofit Management, and New York Theological Seminary, serving as an adjunct professor, program advisor and member of The Board of Trustees.

You shall receive power when the Holy Ghost comes upon you...

OUIDA C. WYATT is a Psalmist, artist and writer on the ministerial staff of The Greater Allen AME Cathedral of New York. She has served as an advisor, speaker and facilitator for Chosen Vessels Girl's Rite of Passage, The Cancer Support Ministry and Marriage Enrichment Ministry. Ouida Wyatt designed and taught a course titled Power of The Pen: Spiritual Growth Through Journaling. She is an honors graduate of the College of New Rochelle, with a B.A. in Psychology and Certified Life Coach. Ouida Wyatt states that her ministry is helping people discover inner peace, power and happiness through a deeper relationship with God and self. Alfonso & Ouida are partners in marriage and ministry for 40 years.

For we have this treasure in earthen vessels...

www.ingramcontent.com/pod-product-compliance
Lightning Source LLC
Chambersburg PA
CBHW031430290426
44110CB00011B/599